Rookie Biographies®

POPE FRANCIS
A Man of Love and Peace

by Marie Morreale

Content Consultant
Nanci R. Vargus, Ed.D.
Professor Emeritus, University of Indianapolis

Reading Consultant
Jeanne M. Clidas, Ph.D.
Reading Specialist

Children's Press®
An Imprint of Scholastic Inc.

Library of Congress Cataloging-in-Publication Data
Names: Morreale, Marie, author.
Title: Pope Francis : a man of love and peace / by Marie Morreale ; poem by
Jodie Shepherd.
Description: New York : Childrens Press, 2016. | Series: Rookie biographies |
Includes bibliographical references and index.
Identifiers: LCCN 2016009003| ISBN 9780531220665 (library binding) |
ISBN 9780531220856 (pbk.)
Subjects: LCSH: Francis, Pope, 1936–Juvenile literature. |
Popes–Biography–Juvenile literature.
Classification: LCC BX1378.7 .M673 2016 | DDC 282.092 [B] –dc23 LC record
available at https://lccn.loc.gov/2016009003

Produced by Spooky Cheetah Press
Poem by Jodie Shepherd

© 2017 by Scholastic Inc.

Printed in China 62

SCHOLASTIC, CHILDREN'S PRESS, ROOKIE BIOGRAPHIES™, and associated logos are
trademarks and/or registered trademarks of Scholastic Inc.

1 2 3 4 5 6 7 8 9 10 R 25 24 23 22 21 20 19 18 17 16

Photographs ©: cover: Vandeville Eric/Newscom; cover background: Jayk67/
Dreamstime; 3 background: SpaceKris/Shutterstock, Inc.; 4-5: Molly Riley/Getty
Images; 6 left: michaklootwijk/Thinkstock; 6 right: MattiaATH/Thinkstock; 8: Franco
Origlia/Getty Images; 9: yevgeniy11/Shutterstock, Inc.; 11: Grupo44/Getty Images;
12: Clarin/Reuters; 13: Franco Origlia/Getty Images; 15: Leonard McCombe/Getty
Images; 16-17: Pablo Leguizamon/AP Images; 19: Alessia Pierdomenico/Shutterstock,
Inc.; 20-21: cesc_assawin/Shutterstock, Inc.; 23: AFP/Getty Images; 24-25: Andreas
Solaro/Getty Images; 27: Michael Appleton/Reuters; 29: giulio napolitano/
Shutterstock, Inc.; 30 background: SpaceKris/Shutterstock, Inc.; 31 top: Africa Studio/
Shutterstock, Inc.; 31 center top: Clarin/Reuters; 31 center bottom: Andrea Danti/
Fotolia; 31 bottom: kaetana/Shutterstock, Inc.; 32 background: Sergii Figurnyi/Fotolia.

Maps by Mapping Specialists

TABLE OF CONTENTS

Meet
Pope Francis

In 2013, Pope Francis became the head of the Roman Catholic Church. As the 266th pope, he also made history. For more than 1,200 years, all of the popes had come from Europe. Francis is the first to be born in the Americas.

Pope Francis was born Jorge Mario Bergoglio on December 17, 1936. He lived in Buenos Aires, Argentina. His grandparents, aunts, uncles, and cousins all lived close by. They often had big family dinners. Jorge loved helping his mom in the kitchen.

FAST FACT!

Collecting stamps was one of Jorge's early hobbies.

Buenos Aires

ARGENTINA

MAP KEY

● City where Pope
  Francis was born

Area enlarged

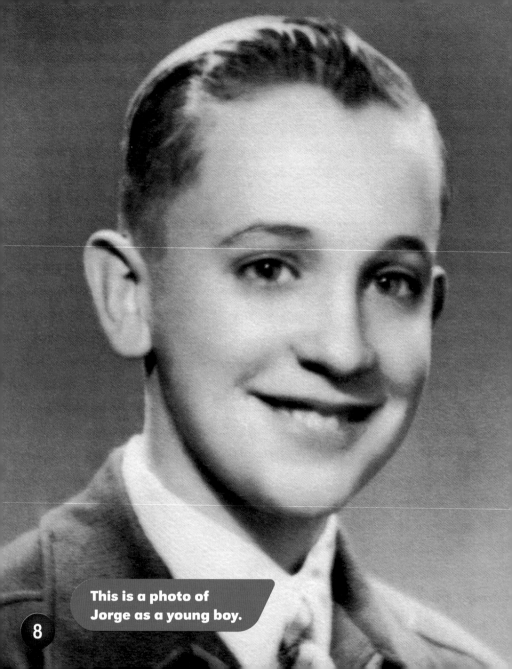

This is a photo of Jorge as a young boy.

Jorge was a very good student. He loved to read. He was also interested in science. For fun, Jorge and his friends went to local soccer matches. He also loved to go dancing. His favorite dance style was the tango.

FAST FACT!

Jorge enjoyed playing soccer with his friends and family.

A New Direction

When he was a teenager, Jorge started thinking about becoming a priest. He wanted to help the poor and sick people in Buenos Aires. When he was 19, he entered the **seminary**. At 21, he joined the Jesuits. They are a teaching order of Catholic priests. They have schools all around the world.

Jorge studied at the Colegio Máximo de San José in Buenos Aires.

Father Bergoglio celebrates a mass.

It takes many years to become a Jesuit. During that time, Jorge taught high school students. Next he taught new Jesuits. In 1969, Jorge was **ordained** a Jesuit priest. He was given the official name Father Bergoglio.

Father Bergoglio

Father Bergoglio continued as a teacher. He also started programs to feed, house, and educate the poor. Then, in the 1980s, he decided to focus on helping those in need. Father Bergoglio believed this was the reason he became a priest. He worked with poor, sick, and elderly people in the town of Córdoba.

Bergoglio worked in Córdoba, which is about a six-hour drive from Buenos Aires.

Most church leaders travel in private cars. Bergoglio liked to ride the subway.

In 2001, Bergogolio was named a cardinal. He was the leader of the church in Argentina. Still, he lived a very simple life. Bergogolio did not live in a large house. He did not have servants. He had his own apartment and cooked for himself. He was not focused on his power in the church. His goal was to care for all the people of Argentina.

In 2005, Pope John Paul II died. One of the duties of a cardinal is to elect the pope. So Bergoglio flew to Rome to cast his **ballot**. Pope Benedict XVI was chosen. Little did Bergoglio know that eight years later he would make the same trip. But there would be a very different result!

FAST FACT!

When Cardinal Bergoglio went to elect Pope Benedict XVI, it was the first time he had ever been to Rome.

Pope Benedict XVI

19

City where Pope
Francis lives

Vatican
City

Vatican City is in Rome.
It is the headquarters
of the Catholic Church.

Changing the World

In 2013, Pope Benedict XVI announced he was retiring. On March 12, tens of thousands of people gathered outside the Vatican. They waited to see who the new pope would be. The next day, on the fifth vote, Cardinal Bergoglio was named pope.

A new pope picks a new name. He usually honors a pope or a **saint**. Bergoglio chose the name Francis. This was to honor Saint Francis of Assisi, who dedicated his life to the poor.

Once again, Francis decided to live simply. The pope usually lives in a palace. Instead, Francis moved into a two-room apartment.

The new pope Francis greets the people who waited for him in St. Peter's Square.

Pope Francis likes to be out among his followers.

Papa Francesco!

The pope is very busy.
He always travels in a special
vehicle called the popemobile.
Francis often gets out of his
car to greet his followers.
He hugs the people—especially
the children. Crowds greet
Pope Francis with cheers of
"Papa Francesco!"

Pope Francis wants to fight poverty, disease, lack of education, and violence around the world. He has traveled to many countries. It is important to him to spread his message of love and peace around the world.

When Pope Francis visited the United States, he led a mass at Madison Square Garden. About 20,000 people attended.

Pope Francis is humble, kind, and loving. He works to help people who need it the most. Francis has millions of followers who adore him. He is an inspiration to people everywhere.

Timeline of Pope Francis's Life

1936	**1958**	**1969**
Born on December 17	Enters the Jesuit seminary	Is ordained a Jesuit priest

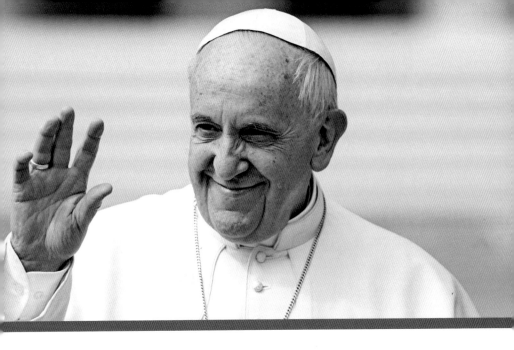

Named cardinal

Makes his first visit as pope to the United States

1998 > **2001** > **2013** > **2015**

Named archbishop of Buenos Aires

Elected pope of the Roman Catholic Church on March 13

A Poem About Pope Francis

Humble to his very core,
fighter for the sick and poor.
Pope Francis is our best reminder
to make the world a little kinder.

You Can Help Others

 Be kind and generous to your family and friends.

 Come up with ideas to help those who have less than you do.

 Find ways to be kind in your community—help an elderly neighbor, for example.

Glossary

ballot (BAL-uht): way of voting secretly

ordained (or-DAYND): made a priest, minister, or rabbi

saint (SAYNT): person who has been officially recognized for living a very holy life, such as Saint Francis of Assisi (*right*)

seminary (SEM-uh-ner-ee): school that trains students to become priests, ministers, or rabbis

Index

Facts for Now

Visit this Scholastic Web site for more information on Pope Francis:
www.factsfornow.scholastic.com
Enter the keywords Pope Francis

About the Author

Marie Morreale is the author of many celebrity biographies. She is also the executive editor, media, of Scholastic Classroom Magazines. Marie did not get to see the pope in person when he was in New York. But she watched him on TV!